At Home

Life with Inspiration and Support from our Creator

P. K. Harris

WALDENHOUSE PUBLISHERS, INC.
WALDEN, TENNESSEE

Photographs by: Fred Harris; Marshall Faintich, birds; Gretchen Griffith, Littlejohn Church
Published by Waldenhouse Publishers, Inc.
100 Clegg Street, Signal Mountain, Tennessee 37377 USA
888-222-8228   www.waldenhouse.com
Printed in the United States of America
Type and Design by Karen Paul Stone
ISBN: 978-1-947589-26-1
Library of Congress Control Number: 2020937040
  Collection of free-verse poems expressing inspiration and courage from our Creator, not only in good times, but also in battling cancer and chemotherapy. Seventy-nine poems and twenty-two color photographs illustrate the resilience and serenity of nature from the Appalachians to Antarctica.
POE000000 POETRY / General
POE023030 POETRY / Subjects & Themes / Nature
POE005010 POETRY / American / General

Dedicated to

The Glory of God
as seen in all of Creation.

Introduction

Relax as you read and "see" the scene
presented in each poem.

Prologue

To see the beauty and peace
which surrounds us in the big out-of-doors as it
brings that same beauty and peace into our lives.
It is a gift from God to accept and enjoy.

Acknowledgments

Annette Miller, Fred Harris, Peter White,
Marshall Faintich, Joyce Knight, Gretchin Griffith
and Karen Stone of Waldenhouse Publishers

Contents

At Home

I am at home in the wild.
I feel a blending of souls.....
Nature and I commune in
our own language.
She accepts me as one
with her. I hear music and
sing in tune and harmony.

Altars

What joy to approach a church altar!
Kneeling before God---feeling
His presence.

Yet, when I sit by a tree,
am I not at an altar?

A strategy to spend time with
God can be anywhere, anytime:
driving a car, washing dishes,
tending a garden. Anywhere!

God is everywhere and in all of
His creation.

All of life is an altar.

Joy in His presence!

Breakfast With Flowers

They greet me as I
enter their space.
A lovely bouquet of
many colors.

The Flowers lift their
soft voices and sing
as I eat my first meal
of the day in their
presence.

So much love and joy
they bring from the
loved ones that sent
them and God who
grew them.

Blessings.

Clouds

Deep blue clouds,
rolling and tumbling
over each other in
joy and laughter,
totally unconcerned
with the deluge
they were dispensing
on the earth below.

On they race until
their moisture is
spent and they give
way to their white
puffy companions
in the sky.

Desert

There are times in my life's
journey when I feel like I'm
walking through a desert
with mirages appearing and
disappearing in my
stressed mind.
Hope of emerging from this
desert seems to be in the
far off "forever".

Yet in my mind,
glimpses begin to appear of
the beauty of this desert.
My, the glory of that cactus
in bloom, and was that a
roadrunner scuttling after
a bug?

The mirages begin appearing in more
form and I see that beauty
surrounds me.
I realize I am totally immersed in it!
My "forever" is right here as
I open my inner eyes.

Desire!

Desire! Pushing, struggling
to be turned loose.
To be free to soak up
life as I desire to feed
my soul.

Is this total selfishness?
Sounds like it,
looks like it.
Yet, it is not my job
to carry another person.

I feel suppressed,
held down by "tradition"
or what society thinks is "right."

Do I just not have the courage
to step out and reclaim my life?

That, too!

How do you feel Inner Self?

Diamonds

Want to be rich? Want diamonds to surround you--
all yours?
Step out into nature's abundance.
A clean, cold morning is offering diamonds on
every twig, stone, and limb as the rising
sun kisses each.

The diamonds are for those who see, those who
partake, those who want to be rich with
nature's gift. And – the diamonds are
totally free!

So, fill your soul to overflowing.
They're all yours!

Early Morning Fog

The early morning fog caresses the meadow
and gently enfolds it to its breast.
Each blade of grass, seed and flower
is softly bathed in the mist
making the entire world a mystery.
The angled disks of meadow spiders,
great creations of nature's art,
watch as the sun punches a blurry hole
in the resistant mist
and creates diamonds on every thread of web.

What glory shines for a brief heartbeat!
The meadow and I are rich with all the wealth--
millions of diamonds just
for our eyes to feast upon.
Rich, blessed, and privileged
to behold such a spectacle!

So quickly and silently the
light chases the fog away.
The meadow and I are left wondering
if we really saw the wondrous sight,
yet know it is etched in our
mind's eye to enjoy again and again.

What marvelous gifts are given
by God's Nature
when our souls take the time
to stop, be still and behold!

Fantastic

Why are you furious with me body?
You have harbored some
very bad critters!

Good thing my angels are alert
and fast to bomb those
critters out of existence.

Fantastic!

Flowering

Boy, I sure like the
feeling when I'm
flowering.
Winter, spring,
summer, fall, I can
flower away in
my soul
because I am
resilient.

No holding me down!
Flowers are like that,
ya know.

They lift the soul no
matter the weather.

Flower on Soul!

Friend

I like that word!
It speaks to me of
laughter,
good conversation,
companionship,
connection,
growing in Spirit.

Wow Friend!
What a gift you are
to me!

Fuzzy Sun

Fuzzy sun peeking through
the early morning fog
lighting up each
dew-soaked
spider web
creating
wood fairies,
ditch fairies,
and
grass fairies.

Gifts of beauty
to begin the day!

Thanks!

Girgle

I was wondering about you
today little stream.
Do you girgle over the
rocks just because
you are small?

What happens to you
after a big rain?
Do you girgle or roar?

Wondering about your life
makes me take close
notice of you.
You keep your secrets well.

I see now taking time
to pay attention to
small things
enriches my life.

Girgle! Girgle!

Giants

Grand, giant trees!
The serenity in the grove
was deep and peaceful.
Living totally in the moment,
accepting life as it is and giving all
to those who come
to partake of their peace.

The alarm chatter of a squirrel
shatters the silence as if the
probing rays of the sun into
the grove had broken into bits
of glass and clattered to the ground.

After all his excited commotion,
the squirrel, satisfied with his
announcement about these biped
intruders, again set about collecting
the giant's grand fruit for winter eating.

Serenity reigned. Twenty-two
paces it took to measure one giant's
base. I hugged it, trying to "hear "
its soft words. Gentle strength flowed
into me and I gave the giant my thanksgiving.

We are one, this giant and I.
Connected in ways I cannot fathom.

Joyous in our relationship.
Both of us are sojourners for a
short while on our earth home,

sharing everything,
including the air we breathe.

How I love the breath of a tree!
Fresh, clean, refreshing to my body and soul.

My heart will walk again among
you, my brothers, no matter
where my body is.
You are now truly a part of me.
Enriching. Calming.

Serenity with the giants.

Going Under

WOW! The lights are so bright here!
Doc must see what he is doing.
Needles, tubes, then fluid.
Is all that going in me?
Arrange my body – arms just so.
Pillows under my knees. Comfy?
Go for it!

Quickly – fuzzy sight.
Then I'm gone.
Where??
Only God knows.

Seconds later – or was it hours?
Voices.
Fuzzy sight again.
I'm back!
Gentle hands minister to me.
Cold water and crackers.
Delicious!
It's been hours since food intake.
Blessings.
Soon mobile, dressed and
out the door.
On the way to healing.
God is still carrying me.

Thank you God!

Gratitude

Up-welling from my Source deep inside.
Life. Smiles. Loving bonds.
New friends.
Wild majestic nature: wild
kisses to match.

All gifts from Love, abundantly given.
Embraced deeply.
Gratitude!

He's Carrying Me

Life changed suddenly from
joy and interesting to
a hard bumpy road.

I know He is always
walking with me.
His presence is felt in my
deep heart.

Now He is carrying me!
There is only one set of
footprints in the sand.

Rejoicing in this knowing,
the hard bumps are smoothing out.
Is life now easy?
NO!
But my strong companion
makes the journey doable.

Thank you for carrying me!

Heart A-Hurtin'

Heart a–hurtin' in the midst of such beauty?
Why?
Is the magnificence of nature
so overwhelming that
it makes my heart hurt?

Nature's beauty envelops me
with soft loving eyes and eager searching lips
that shares passion with me
like a hot summer breeze,
refreshing as a soft rain.

Be gentle with my heart,
you wild son of nature.
Hold me in your beauty.
Fill me with your fire.
Consume me until we are one
and my heart is a–hurtin' no more.

Hidden Diamonds

In the stillness of the deep, dark,
hidden places in Mother Earth you
are formed.

You are content for eons of time
in your dark womb. Then a
thought enters your diamond heart.
Sun light you crave to show
your real beauty.
You must sparkle and shine!

There is a diamond hidden in the
stillness of me.
Spirit!
It, too, yearns for the sunlight.
Only when the light rays shine on
and out of my diamond Spirit can
it come to life.

Us diamonds must stick together and
bring sun light and joy to all we
shine upon.

So, shine on Diamonds!

His Majesty

The waves roll onto shore,
one after the other,
endlessly.

Mighty.
Uncontrollable.

Man is mere nothing before
this majesty
of the sea.

Yet, though like specks
of sand on the beach,
HE loves us.

Unconditionally.

Mystery!

Majesty!

Hooked Up!

Today is the day!
No more waiting.
It's staring me in the face.
Poison must flow
into my body.
The critters must
be wiped out!

Tears flow.
I read, "There is no
situation that Spirit
and I cannot move
through with
love and ease."

Ease??? Not sure
about that!
But, we will make it,
Spirit and I.

Hot Diggety Dog

Total strangers, these two pups.
Wow! All new smells!
Sniff! Sniff!
Checking each other out.

Released from leashes,
joyous running, circling,
nipping and barking.
Marking all posts near and far.
More sniffing.

Ball chasing, treats, petting
and "good boys" amid
laughter from the spectators.

Play time, fun and new friends made,
until another day to run and play again.

Howling

Do you howl at the moon?
What fun!
Cut to the chase--
waste not a minute.

The moon is waiting to hear you howl.
The stars like it too.

Music to their ears.
When you howl at them they
know you are sending
them love.

So, howl some more!

Joy!

Joy, Joy, Joy!

Whoops!
Crash!
Catastrophe!

Life changed.
Bummer!

But then, blessings
quickly began
showing up.

WOW! No idea a
crash could
produce all this

Joy! Joy! Joy!

Journey of Leaves

There is a tiny stream hidden deep in the forest.
It winds its way slowly, but deliberately, past
trees and bushes which are its neighbors.

During autumn when the leaves gain their color,
then finally turn loose of their twigs and drift down,
many fall onto this tiny stream.

Some leaves get caught in eddies,
and others catch on limbs and rocks.
The adventurous leaves get into the main current and
slowly begin their journey to see the world
on the back of the tiny stream.

As I contemplate on this union of leaves and water,
I see my life reflected in the leaf journeys.
Many times I've been in eddies or stuck on rocks
and going nowhere. Then "something" shoves me
out into the current. Fear may rule for a while,
but as the journey progresses the joy of
the adventure lifts me to new heights.

Why did I resist the "current" so long?
What wondrous things I am seeing
and experiencing!

Now, Faith in knowing I am cared for and
totally guided in the "current" gives
me joy and peace.

What a journey!

Knock! Knock!

Knock! Knock! Who's there?
Is this a real question?
It's ME who is knocking!

Knocking is my way of drawing
you out of your hiding place.
Are you stuck in there?

Knock. Knock. Come on out so
we can share who we really are.
You can always go back into your
hiding place. But, maybe, if you
come out into the sunshine you
may not want to go back in that place.

Let's ask each other questions and
take the adventure on from there.

OK??

Knock! Knock!

Little Weeds

Big weeds, easy to see,
but hard to uproot.

Little weeds, ignored
sometimes to become
big weeds.

I wonder?

How many little "weeds"
do I ignore in my heart
until they become
big "weeds"?

Jesus has a spade
that can uproot
them all.

Forgiveness!!

Light On A Hill

From an early brush arbor in 1775,
you have been a beacon on the hill top.
Countless souls have found a peacefulness
within your walls whether of brush,
logs or frame.

Circuit riders ministered to families
and nourished the church through many
decades. From a meeting house you
became Littlejohn Church.

Your lofty rafters have rung with joyful
hymns and softened the sorrows and
griefs of heavy hearts.

You spawned many souls who were
obedient to God's call of service and
sent them out as ambassadors in
all walks of life.

On your grassy knoll, many loved ones
lie at peace while their souls are held
in the arms of Jesus.

Now well into your third century you are
still a light on the hill welcoming any
and all souls seeking God's
peace and love.

Lookout Sunshine!

Here comes Evil with some of his
buddies: fear, darkness, violence
and hate.
Evil thinks he can take over and
rule. He hasn't yet discovered that
he doesn't exist, except in the hearts
of those who have closed their
eyes to Sunshine.

Sunshine patiently waits—forever if
necessary. When hearts get weary from
struggling through darkness and all
the joy has been sucked out
of their life, maybe, just maybe,
their eyes can see a tiny shaft of
Sunshine filtering through
the darkness.

How good that must feel! For that
tiny shaft can warm that peace-starved
heart. Joy and love flow in.
The heart slowly remembers.
This is its true nature.

Bathe daily in the Sunshine.
It's free, unlimited abundance!
All yours to enjoy!

Memories

The place is so familiar.
I've been here many times.
Yet, this time memories
flood my mind and heart.

The music is still here,
but my friends are gone.
Dancing, laughter, friendship.
They were so alive then!
Ouch! How my heart hurts!

Maybe when I go too, we
will meet on the other side
and dance again to God's
music.

Meditation

Stilling my mind and soul is
spending time with my Maker,
I meditate.

When I commune with Nature,
I meditate.

When I sit quietly and
watch ocean waves break
on shore,
I meditate.

When I spend time with
a dear friend,
I meditate.

When I connect in awe with
a wild flower,
I meditate.

When I gaze on lofty mountains
in appreciation of their beauty,
I meditate.

When I breathe the breath
of the trees,
I meditate.

When I see the manifestation
of God in all things,
I meditate.

When I am in peace, joy,
and love,
I meditate

I find all of life is a continuous
meditation.

Morning Mist

A fresh washed world!
What – who is hiding
in the mist?

Oh my! Trees--
and all of Nature
drinking in the
Creator's abundance.

Me too? Yes!
Enjoying all the glory
of the morning.

Blessed me!!

Morning Music

©Marshall Faintich

Early morning light.
Brain and body still
drugged with sleep.
But music is coming
from somewhere.

Oh Joy!

It's the feathered songsters
outside!
Wren and cardinal welcoming
the new day with
their joyous anthem.

God's voice singing
a duet.

Warm bed!
Beautiful music!

©Marshall Faintich

Blessings!

Mr. Woolly Worm

I met a woolly worm today.
He was on a mission from
somewhere to somewhere else.

Rock, grass, obstacles – no problem!
He took them all in stride.
Occasionally a smell made him
pause to investigate, then
on he went.

Mr. Woolly had a purpose
in mind. Nothing made
him pause for long.

A lesson for me?

Yep!

Nectar From Heaven

Dry!
Desert mouth!
Four days,
no water!

Then, miracle!
A cup of ice chips
arrive.

Hand reaches out,
fingers grasp the spoon,
nectar from Heaven
falls into my mouth.
Joy! Celebration!

Cold moisture
swishes all
around my mouth, then
cascades down my dry
throat, where the stomach pump whisks
it away.
But
I had the Nectar of Heaven.
Ice Chips!

Oceans And Seas

Always desiring to move.

Always fulfilling that desire.

Restless.

Whispering of things seen and unseen.

Mystery!

Intrigue!

Awesome!

Peaceful at times, but
deep emotions which
spill out in
magnificent rage.

Unspeakable beauty
in peace or rage.

Untamed! Untamable!
Like my Spirit!

Made of the same God Stuff!

Magnificent!

Out Of The Pit

The news was not good!

Shock and disbelief threw
me in a deep, dark pit.

It's strange how a few words
can put out the sunlight.

Tears flowed.

God was here somewhere
in this darkness, but
I couldn't find His hand.

I grouped---searching.

Family, friends and Drs. Katz and Buck
brought flashlights.
Angels stirred.

Finally, after being nurtured and
hugged, out the top of the pit
I crawled.
My hand had found His!

The sun felt so grand!
The darkness was gone.

My soul is again filled with
The Light and I am
rejoicing in His
abundant Goodness.

Peeking Out

My Soul peeks out my window.
WOW! There's lots of space
out there!

Out the door, on the porch,
past the flowers, down the
steps to the fork
in the road.

To the sunrise or sunset?
Why not both in their
own time!

Can't waste all
that space. No more
peeking out my
window.

My Soul loves all that space!

Perfect Bliss

When I become still and quiet
and go inside where Spirit lives,
and commune in that solitude,
perfect bliss.

When I see, feel and share the
manifestations of Spirit in
Nature,
perfect bliss.

When the chaos of the world
roils and boils around me,
I know that quiet place
with Spirit awaits inside
to welcome me.

Perfect bliss!

Port Out!

The Big C elephant in the room
was knocked down several notches!

Unburdened! Fresh air!

Stepping out on Faith, knowing
my capable Companion will see
me through all the moments
of my life.

Joy!

Rapturous Song

Quiet, peaceful.

Suddenly,
A rapturous song!
Mr. Wren is singing
to a glorious morning.

Small body, with his tiny
beak saluting the sky,
he belts out his song
for all to hear.

What a joy!
Thank you God
for this gift that
adds another
blessing to my
day!

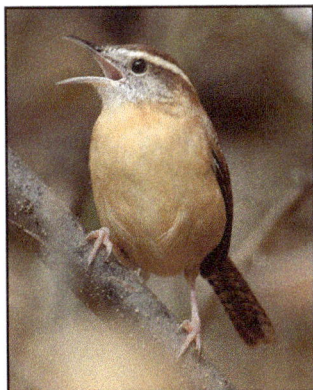

Carolina Wren © Marshall Faintich

Remission

A beautiful word to celebrate!
After a long siege, remission,
relief, joy, renewed strength.

Rejoice long!
Relax deeply in His
Grace and Love.

Thank you God!!!

Restless Seas

Oh my, you restless seas!
You taste this shore and
that shore.
What are you searching for?
New and different experiences?
Are you looking for a home?

You are like my soul – always searching.
My soul tastes of many ideas, insights,
and inspirations – all so interesting.

But mostly my soul is searching
for home.
It's up ahead somewhere
on God's time.
There it will be restless no more.

Restless

Restless! Restless!
Oh, my soul.
Yearning, seeking
Child of God.

Roaming the mountains
and valleys of my
heart.
Making footprints on my
ribs and mind
as I seek to find and
satisfy this hunger of
my Soul.

Light! There is Light!
Gently beckoning me
to follow.
The Light is Love.
The Light is Peace.
My Soul wants to feed on it.

Consume this restless, seeking
Soul, Warm Light.
Fill my hunger.
My Soul is love-starved.
Hold me. Cradle me.
Satisfy this restless Soul!

Ridin' High

The call came loud and clear.
My ears immediately knew what they were hearing.
High above against the deep blue sky
sailed three red-tailed hawks.
Joined by a vulture, they were
riding a high thermal.

Around and around they swooped and
floated – joyous in their freedom to fly.

My whole being joined them
and my soul felt the joy of embracing
the gifts of sun, breeze, and
sharpened senses.

We sailed a while, the birds and I,
and for long after, I smiled
and felt the joy of soaring high.

©Marshall Faintich

Riding The Wind

Oh, how wonderful!
The wind is softly rustling in the trees.
Where did it come from and where is it going?

Wouldn't it be fun and adventurous to vanish from
where I am now rooted and ride the wind!
What would I behold and as I learned more
of the wind's life and journey,
what beliefs would I discard or cultivate?
Would I ever want to be "rooted" again?
Would I be the same person as before?

I would think not!

After all, when you have ridden the wind
into the rainbow and stayed until it vanished,
your belief in God and life would be forever changed.

Rim

Up on the rim
of a canyon.
Lovely view especially
with the glow of
sunset.

Hummmm.

Sure wish I knew
how to get down!

Safety?

Most folks are not willing to
step out in life. Safety!
That is their goal.

Wild Nature is in my Soul.
No wishful thinking for me.

Out the door!

Look out world! This wild
Soul is on the move!

Separation

Separation! My group! Your group!
World, you have to be totally crazy to
make us feel this way.

But, World, you are made up of
us – groups, clubs, religions.

Boy, you look different from me.
I look at you and feel fear,
distrust, and that awful word,
separation.

How can, when can, we ever
see we are all brothers and
sisters?

Look out World! I'm out to
change my outlook. Maybe
the next "you" I meet can begin
to see my new outlook
and take up the change also.

Here we come World! Get ready!

Oneness is on the way!

Serenity

In the garden of serenity
deep inside of me is a place of
peace, love and joy.

This garden awaits me
and longs for me to leave
the dramas of the world
and spend time in
this quiet place.

There is always a joyous welcome
as I tread softly into the garden
and commune with God.

Refreshed after each visit to the garden,
I face the world's dramas with
calm assurance that God is by
my side – always!

Life is for my highest good.

All is Well!

She

SHE is sunshine.

SHE is joy.

SHE is love.

SHE is innocence.

SHE is giggles and laughter.

SHE is music to the heart.

SHE is a woodland fairy.

SHE is quiet.

SHE is peace.

SHE is steady and faithful.

SHE is a gift from God to the world.

SHE is my daughter.

She's Just Down The Path

Her soul will walk the earth no more,
but her joy and laughter will remain
in our hearts.

Wonderful friendships and great
accomplishments are her legacy.
She was a huge soul in a
tiny package.

She is out of sight, but just down the path,
very alive, smiling, and waiting
to greet her loved ones as their
journeys on earth are completed.

Cheers to a great lady!
She is loved and missed.

Our Anne

Shells

Shells, by the millions on the sand.
Broken, yet exquisite in design
by our Creator.

Just like us humans!

Silence

Leave noise behind.
Get lost in the beauty
of Nature.
Instead of reading about God,
look at the face of God
in Nature's silence.

Trees speak in soft silent tones
straight to the heart.
Joy sings from the movement
of a breeze in grass.
Waves roar onto the beach
and roll in silence over the
weary soul and bring peace.

The still small voice of God
can be heard in silence.
All gifts given from our
God of love.

Sky

Early morning. Sunrise.
Mr. Sun announces himself
long before he shows his face.
Turquoise and pink, then yellow
and orange. He paints the
sky with a lavish brush.

Attention! Attention!
Mr. Sun moves on swiftly and
takes the colors with him
to those down the path
watching and waiting for
him and the gift of
another day.

Sliding

WOW! I feel I am sliding through life.
Survival is my goal.
But, life is so much more than
just survival.

Survival is like a leaky fountain. Soon there
is no water to splash with joy.

I crave all the ups and downs of life.
Variety, adventure, growth of
mind and spirit.

No more just sliding, unless
it is into something exciting!

Snow

All of nature seems to be holding its breath
awaiting the first flakes of snow.

As the gathering flakes caress the land,
all the scars we have inflicted on the earth
disappear in a clean fresh coat of white.

Stillness reigns, the pace of life slows
and for a short time souls can take
a breath from all the busyness
imposed on them.

Oh that we could stay in this state!
To slow down and enjoy the blessings
heaped upon us. No rushing here
and there for more-more-more.

Accept the gift of snow.
Allow it to cover all your scars.
Enjoy your new clean fresh coat.

Snow And Ice

Rough, craggy mountains who live
with snow and ice all their lives.
Glaciers flowing like
hard white rivers.

Birds that waddle, but do not
fly except under water.
Curious they are as they
welcome us into their
nesting grounds.
Eyeing us, trying to place these
strange looking penguins that
have entered their world.

Sleeping giants! Elephant seals
looking like beached whales
on shore.

Beach Master fur seals guarding
their tiny territories on black beaches
waiting to capture females coming
ashore to birth more of their kind.

Birds! Oh my! Those albatross
with ten foot wings soaring over the
seas! They and other birds that come
to land only to nest.

Whales spouting welcome plumes teasing
us who so want to make their
acquaintance, but they are shy
and return to the depths.

Mysterious ice bergs of all sizes and shapes,
some sporting ancient blue ice.

Silent, majestic, forbidding, yet alluring.
Totally hostile, but
beautiful beyond words.

Antarctica!

Solace

Solace. What is solace?
Does it appear softly
or does it knock you
over as it enters the
window?

Where it comes from
or how it appears,
I don't know.
But – it sounds
easy, comforting.

Can words like solace
do that?
Of course they can.

So, whatever you are
solace, come on.
I'm waiting for you!

Speed Bumps

Flying high in the sky
where no clouds or eagles fly.
Joyously smooth sailing!
Suddenly, bumpity, bumpity, bumpity!

No need to worry.
These are only speed bumps
in the sky.

Spirit

Spirit, are you the one who is
walking on the floors and
ceilings of my heart?
What are you
searching for?
Are you lost and
looking for home?

Searching? Yes!
Lost? No!

Spirit, you know where
home is. It is with HIM.

This you know and the
rest of me is learning.
Lead me on this path
with trust and joy.

Help my heart and mind
to keep step with your
restless pacing.

How much longer will
you pace before
going home?

Only HE knows!

Suds!

Warm, soapy suds
all over my body.
Luxurious shower, even alone.
Yet, something--someone is missing.
YOU!

Join me as I share my suds with you.
Gently giving to each other.
Smooth wet skin to
smooth wet skin.
Together in our shower of bliss.

Soft, loving, gentle, making sweet
memories to share for a lifetime.

Oh, the joy of shared suds!

The Bestest And Swiftest

Those rancher cowboys come a gallopin'!
Ride 'um, rope 'um.
Into the trailer wild steer.

Opps! Missed!

Chase 'um, rope 'um.
Try again.
Good horses, dusty cowboys.
Job done.

Thumbs up for the
bestest and the swiftest.

The Hay Field

Glorious space! Rich grass stretching out with
the big bowl of sky over me.
I am held, wrapped in Peace and Quiet.

The sky is always a joy. Sometimes white
puffy clouds reign, benign and quiet;
sometimes deep blue storm clouds, rolling
and tumbling in majesty; sometimes
just nothing but sunshine to caress me.

Here in the hay field the birds serenade me, the
wind woos me with love songs and my
soul is refreshed.

Here I linger, savoring, storing up the
sweetness of each moment as my
soul remembers that this peace
and joy is my natural place.

This hay field is always in my heart so I can
step into it in a heartbeat to be
held in Peace and Quiet.

The Cabin

How content you are to
look at the majesty of God
in the landscape before you.

You live quietly through the seasons
with your native neighbors of
birds, deer, elk and bear.

Your structure is of wood
from living trees. You have
taken on their life and share
with all who come through
your door.

You are a haven for soul-
weary travelers. Here in your peace
the hassles of life can fall away,
joy is restored, lives mended,
Spirit inside found again.

How privileged I am to
received your peace as I
linger for a while within you.
With a heart full of gratitude and
joy, I will step once more into
the outer world, knowing I can
always return in my mind to be
renewed by the gifts of your
peace and solitude.

The Leaf

In early, early spring, before
old man winter had released
his grip on the land, a tiny
leaf bud was born on the twig of a tree.

The tiny bud was curled tightly against
the chill, but was aware of the
new life stirring within its veins.

As the sun warmed and softly
kissed the tiny bud, it trusted
its Source for continued nourishment and
slowly began to grow, then cautiously
unfurl. Wow! The release of the tight curl
felt so freeing that soon the leaf burst
forth to totally greet life.

What joy the leaf felt as it danced
in the wind, rain, and summer days.
No thought or fear of tomorrow was
in the leaf heart because of the abundant
Source that provided all that was needed.

Day and night flowed by as the leaf allowed
the Source to bring it to its full beauty to
share with all its world.

Soon the leaf felt a new stirring within
as it changed into an autumn dress
even more beautiful than the summer one had been.
Now as the sun caressed it the leaf's new color
gleamed as it continued to dance to its
own life's beat.

Days shortened, the sun's warmth
slowly cooled and the leaf became
very sleepy. Dreamland called and the leaf,
in total trust, turned loose from the twig.
It rode its friend, the wind, to the ground
to awaken to life anew.

The Leafless Trees

It's late autumn and there you stand with
all your glorious summer green and fall colors gone.

Yet your symmetry is stunning!
Your trunk and many limbs speak of life,
though many may think you dead.

But for now, you have withdrawn into yourself
to rest and refresh in total harmony with nature.

When the warm sun of spring awakens you,
you will burst forth in a vibrant
celebration of color and life.

Thank you for teaching me a priceless
lesson of rest and refreshing,
so we can both burst forth
in the celebration of the lives
we are given.

The Opening

The opening in the forest
carried mystery and
excitement.

Just as it spoke to me,
its charming ways
spilled onto my
senses.

Quiet, peace, solitude.
What a charming opening!

The Wink

My heart longed
to travel, but hope
for that was slim.

Then a wink from
the sky sent me
down the path.

Look out world!
Here I come!

Tired

Tired of struggling against my emotions and needs.
Desire for freedom.
Freedom from what?
Can't change my emotions – or can I?

Tried, but my inner self keeps coming to the
surface to remind me of my loneliness.
Loneliness in a relationship?

Yes, big time?

Where will my struggle end?

Only God knows!

Trembling Hands

Hands, why do you tremble? Do you have
a problem I don't know about?
Talk to me, Hands. Tell me what's
on your mind.

Oh, I see! You miss making
mud pies. Well, together we
can fix that!

Let's make something useful
with our mud pies.
How about a brick? How
about lots of bricks?

No more tremble. Now you're happy.

We need to play in the mud more often!

Voice Mail

Hello Voice Mail!
Do you have a heart?
How about a soul?
Are you like a grandfather I
never knew?

Let's arrange a meeting.
Maybe a lovely place
in cyber space.
Is tea served in cyber space?
I'll have green tea with
lemon, please.

See you there Voice Mail.

What a Journey!

Recover!   Re-vision!
I like those words.
They make me smile.

Re-vision makes me
look at each day---
make the day real no
matter the situation.

Thankfulness is the key
to all of life.
Blessings abound.
What a journey!

Whisper of Lace

There was just a whisper of lace-
then she was there.
What thrills will he find
with her?

They speak in whispers.
It keeps the night soft.

The moon smiles as the
lace softly drifts to
the ground.

Whisper to me again,
my Love.

Wild Thing

Out in the wild I always
feel magical.

I can fly with the birds, chase
from tree to tree
with squirrels, sing to the
top of my lungs as birds sing.

I am part of God's creation
and can do anything by
mind, heart and soul.

I'm a wild thing!

Win Or Lose

The cowboys used to be
a wandering bunch.
They liked to win at poker
and rib the loser.

The same was on the
back of a bronc.
Some days they were
the loser in the dirt
with the horse
grinning down at them.

Other times they win
and ride away with
a smile plastered
across their face.

All in all, it was
just life.

Windows

There are many windows through
which I look as I make my
journey on earth. But, windows
sometimes keeps me in.

Maybe, if I open a door and
enter into another dimension
I may find a whole new world.
I can use my imagination to first
step through the door and
then listen intently to what
I might hear.

But, wouldn't it be more fun to
just step through, enter the
other world and listen in person?

Oh my, why did I stay behind
those windows so long?
Now I have many more windows
to peek into and listen for sounds
coming from the other side.

As a matter of fact, good-by
windows, hello open doors!

Enter, Listen, Enjoy!

Wonder

As I wonder through the cathedrals
of forest and fields, I feel the majesty
of nature around me.

I wonder what stories each entity
could tell me if it could speak.

Yet, they do speak as I peer
into each tiny window of
personality, be it tree,
flower, animal or bird.

Even rocks have a story to tell.

Fascinating!

You're Welcome

From the mountains to the ocean.
It was a long journey.

The last pale rays of the setting
sun were soft in the western sky.
Dusk settled on the waves crashing
onto the beach.

Thankfulness filled my heart for
a safe journey and the
beauty before me.

Suddenly, my eyes saw fire! A
meteorite streaking from the
sky, disintegrating into small
pieces, and going out
just above the water.

"You're welcome," He said!

Bickham Script and Warnock on LSI 70# archivaal white
Type and Design by Karen Paul Stone